# COOL
## PICNICS &
## ROAD FOOD

Beyond the Basics for Kids Who Cook

LISA
WAGNER

A Division of ABDO
**ABDO**
Publishing Company

Visit us at www.abdopublishing.com

Published by ABDO Publishing Company, P.O. Box 398166, Minneapolis, MN 55439. Copyright ©2014 by Abdo Consulting Group, Inc. International copyrights reserved in all countries. No part of this book may be reproduced in any form without written permission from the publisher. The Checkerboard Library™ is a trademark and logo of ABDO Publishing Company.

Printed in the United States of America,
North Mankato, Minnesota
102013
012014

 PRINTED ON RECYCLED PAPER

Editor: Liz Salzmann
Content Developer: Nancy Tuminelly
Cover and Interior Design and Production:
Colleen Dolphin, Mighty Media, Inc.
Food Production: Desirée Bussiere
Photo Credits: Colleen Dolphin, Shutterstock

Library of Congress Cataloging-in-Publication Data
Wagner, Lisa, 1958- author.
  Cool picnics & road food : beyond the basics for kids who cook / Lisa Wagner.
    pages cm. -- (Cool young chefs)
  Audience: Ages 8 to 12.
  Includes index.
  ISBN 978-1-62403-089-5
1.  Picnics--Juvenile literature. 2.  Cooking, American--Juvenile literature. I. Title. II. Title: Cool picnics and road food.
  TX823.W27 2014
  642.3--dc23
                        2013022524

## TO ADULT HELPERS

Congratulations on being the proud parent of an up-and-coming chef! This series of books is designed for children who have already done some cooking—most likely with your guidance and encouragement. Now, with some of the basics out of the way, it's time to really get cooking!

The focus of this series is on parties and special events. The "Big Idea" is all about the creative side of cooking (mastering a basic method or recipe and then using substitutions to create original recipes). Listening to your young chef's ideas for new creations and sharing your own ideas and experiences can lead to exciting (and delicious) discoveries!

While the recipes are designed to let children cook independently as much as possible, you'll need to set some ground rules for using the kitchen, tools, and ingredients. Most importantly, adult supervision is a must whenever a child uses the stove, oven, or sharp tools. Look for these symbols:

Your assistance, patience, and praise will pay off with tasty rewards for the family, and invaluable life skills for your child. Let the adventures in cooking beyond the basics begin!

# CONTENTS

# HOST A PERFECT PICNIC!

Welcome to Cool Young Chefs! If you have already used other Cool Cooking books, this series is for you. You know how to read a recipe and how to prepare ingredients. You have learned about measuring, cooking tools, and kitchen safety. Best of all, you like to cook!

Your kitchen is in the house, but you can serve a meal anywhere. Everything seems to taste better when you eat outside! It is a lot of fun to make a meal to go. This book will teach you how to be a chef on the go!

## WHAT'S IN THE BASKET?

Keep picnic supplies in a basket, tote bag, or box. When it's time for a picnic, you will be ready to go! Here are some things to include.

- paper or plastic plates
- paper or plastic cups
- forks, spoons, and knives
- serving spoons
- napkins
- paper **towels**
- hand wipes
- plastic bags for **garbage**
- blanket or sheet

## MAKE SOME FOOD

Use the recipes in this book to create a very cool picnic! **Dessert** is easy. Just bring slices of watermelon or other fresh fruit.

## FILL THE COOLER & GO!

If your picnic is not in your own yard, you will need a cooler. A hard-sided cooler filled with ice or freezer packs works best. You can freeze juice boxes to use as both ice and drinks. Cold cans of soda or bottled water also help keep food cool.

# WHAT'S THE BIG IDEA?

Besides being a good cook, a chef is prepared, **efficient**, organized, resourceful, creative, and adventurous. The Big Idea in *Cool Picnics & Road Food* is all about being resourceful.

When you make use of ingredients you already have, you are being resourceful. You will also be able to make one recipe many different ways. Now that's cool cooking!

Some of the recipes in this book let you choose your own ingredients. Look for lists of **options** in the ingredients. You do not need to use them all! The idea is to choose a combination of items from the list. This lets you be creative and resourceful.

Here is how it works. The recipe calls for "3 cups vegetables." This is followed by a list of vegetables. The list tells you how to prepare each vegetable for the recipe. You can choose to use 3 cups of one vegetable. Or, you can choose three vegetables and use 1 cup of each. You could even choose six vegetables and use ½ cup of each. When possible, use ingredients you have before you buy anything else. You will save time, money, and you won't waste anything.

# FIRST THINGS FIRST

A successful chef is smart, careful, and patient. Take time to review the basics before you start cooking. After that get creative and have some fun!

## BE SMART, BE SAFE

- Start with clean hands, tools, and work surfaces.
- Always get **permission** to use the kitchen, cooking tools, and ingredients.
- Ask an adult when you need help or have questions.
- Always have an adult nearby when you use the stove, oven, or sharp tools.
- Prevent accidents by working slowly and carefully.

## NO GERMS ALLOWED

After you handle raw eggs or raw meat, wash your hands with soap and water. Wash tools and work surfaces with soap and water too. Raw eggs and raw meat have bacteria that don't survive when the food is cooked. But the bacteria can survive at room or body temperature. These bacteria can make you very sick if you consume them. So, keep everything clean!

## BE PREPARED

- Read through the entire recipe before you do anything else!
- Gather all the tools and ingredients you will need.
- Wash fruits and vegetables well. Pat them dry with a **towel**.
- Get the ingredients ready. The list of ingredients tells how to prepare each item.
- If you see a word you don't know, check the **glossary** on page 30.
- Do the steps in the order they are listed.

## GOOD COOKING TAKES TIME

- Allow plenty of time to prepare your recipes.
- Be patient with yourself. **Prep** work can take a long time at first.

## ONE LAST THING

- When you are done cooking wash all the dishes and **utensils**.
- Clean up your work area and put away any unused ingredients.

8

# KEY SYMBOLS

In this book, you will see some symbols beside the recipes. Here is what they mean.

The recipe requires the use of a stove or oven. You need adult **supervision** and assistance.

A sharp tool such as a peeler, knife, or **grater** is needed. Be extra careful, and get an adult to stand by.

## BEYOND COOL

Remember the Big Idea? In the Beyond Cool boxes, you will find ideas to help you create your own recipes. Once you learn a recipe, you will be able to make many **versions** of it. Remember, being able to make original recipes turns cooks into chefs!

When you modify a recipe, be sure to write down what you did. If anyone asks for your recipe, you will be able to share it proudly.

## GET THE PICTURE

When a step number in a recipe has a circle around it with an arrow, it will point to the picture that shows how to do the step.

③ ⟶

## COOL TIP

These tips can help you do something faster, better, or more easily.

# UNIQUELY COOL

Here are some of the **techniques** and ingredients used in this book.

## TECHNIQUES:

### SEED A CUCUMBER

Use a vegetable peeler to remove the peel. Trim off the ends and cut the cucumber in half the long way. Scrape the seeds out with a spoon.

### CUT THE KERNELS OFF CORNCOBS

Hold a corncob upright on a cutting board. Cut down the side of the cob with a sharp knife. Turn the cob and cut again. Repeat until you've gone all the way around the cob.

### MAKE PERFECT HARD-BOILED EGGS

Put the eggs in a saucepan and cover with cold water. Bring the water to a boil. Cover the pan and remove it from the heat. Let it sit 13 minutes. Then rinse the eggs under cold water until they are cool. The eggs must be cool for the shell to peel off easily.

# INGREDIENTS:

BLACK BEANS

CHILE
POWDER

CILANTRO

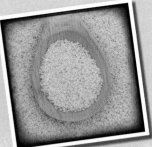

COUSCOUS

CUMIN

FARFELLE

FUSILLI

MOZZARELLA

BREAD
CRUMBS

PENNE

PROVOLONE

SCALLIONS

11

# ANYTHING GOES PASTA SALAD

## ingredients

8 ounces pasta (choose from farfalle, fusilli, or penne)

olive oil

4 ounces mozzarella cheese, cut in ½-inch cubes

3 cups vegetables (options)

- broccoli florets
- cauliflower florets
- sliced carrots
- chopped celery
- sliced radishes
- cherry tomatoes
- cubed zucchini or yellow squash
- chopped red or green bell peppers
- fresh peas
- chopped, peeled, and seeded cucumber
- chopped scallions
- chopped red onion
- pitted black olives
- green olives

double batch of Simple Vinaigrette (see page 13)

salt and pepper

## tools

sharp knife

cutting board

measuring cups & spoons

whisk

large saucepan

strainer

mixing bowls

mixing spoon

plastic wrap

**OPTIONAL**

Add 1 cup salami or pepperoni, cut into cubes or small slices

1. Cook the pasta according to directions on the package. Drain and rinse the pasta. Put it in a large mixing bowl and **drizzle** olive oil over it. Toss to coat the pasta with olive oil.

2. Add the cheese and vegetables and about 1 cup of Simple Vinaigrette.

3. Mix until everything is well coated with vinaigrette. Add more vinaigrette if needed. Add salt and pepper to taste.

4. Cover the bowl with plastic wrap and refrigerate for at least 4 hours before serving.

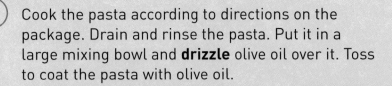

## SIMPLE VINAIGRETTE

**MAKES ABOUT 1 CUP**

ingredients
1/3 cup red wine vinegar

1 teaspoon dried or 1 tablespoon fresh herbs (choose from parsley, oregano, dill, basil, marjoram, and thyme)

1 clove garlic, minced

2/3 cup olive oil

salt and pepper

1. Combine the vinegar, herbs, and garlic in a small bowl.

2. Whisk in the olive oil. If the **dressing** is too sour, add a little more olive oil.

3. Add salt and pepper to taste.

# CLASSIC MACARONI SALAD

MAKES
4 CUPS

## ingredients

16 ounces elbow macaroni

1 tablespoon olive oil

1 small onion, finely chopped

2 stalks celery, finely chopped

1 cup mayonnaise

3 tablespoons white vinegar

1 tablespoon yellow mustard

1 teaspoon salt

½ teaspoon black pepper

4 hard-boiled eggs, peeled and chopped (see page 10)

3 tablespoons chopped fresh parsley or chives

salt and pepper

paprika (optional)

## tools

measuring spoons

measuring cups

sharp knife

cutting board

saucepans with lids

strainer

mixing bowls

mixing spoon

whisk

plastic wrap

1. Cook the macaroni according to directions on the package. Drain and rinse the macaroni. Shake the strainer to remove excess water. Put the macaroni in a large mixing bowl. Add the olive oil and toss to coat. Let the macaroni cool.

2. Add the onion and celery. Mix well.

3. Whisk the mayonnaise, vinegar, mustard, salt, and pepper together in a small mixing bowl. Pour it over the macaroni and vegetables. Mix well. Make sure everything is well coated.

4. Gently stir in the chopped eggs and fresh herbs. Add salt and pepper to taste. Cover the bowl with plastic wrap and refrigerate for at least 3 hours before serving. Just before serving, mix it again. Sprinkle paprika on top if you like.

## BEYOND COOL

- Add a 6-ounce can of drained, rinsed tuna or chicken to the macaroni salad. If it needs more **dressing**, add a little mayonnaise.

- Add 1 cup fresh or frozen peas. If the peas are frozen, toss them into the pot with the macaroni about 2 minutes before the macaroni will be done. Drain the peas and macaroni together.

- Substitute 1½ cups cubed cooked ham for the eggs.

# FRESH COUSCOUS SALAD

## ingredients

2 cups chicken or vegetable broth

2 cups couscous

2 tablespoons olive oil

6 scallions, sliced

1 cucumber, peeled, seeded, and chopped (see page 10)

24 cherry tomatoes, halved

1 red or green bell pepper, chopped

8 radishes, sliced

Simple Vinaigrette (see page 13)

¼ cup chopped parsley

salt and pepper

## tools

measuring cups

measuring spoons

sharp knife

serrated knife

cutting board

medium saucepan with lid

fork

large mixing bowl

mixing spoon

plastic wrap

16

1. Bring the broth to a boil in a medium saucepan. Remove from heat and mix in the couscous. Cover the pan and let it sit for 10 minutes.

2. **Drizzle** the olive oil over the couscous and **fluff** it with a fork. Put the couscous in a large mixing bowl. Let it cool.

3. Stir the vegetables into the couscous.

4. Add the vinaigrette and mix well to coat. Gently stir in the chopped parsley. Add salt and pepper to taste.

5. Cover the bowl with plastic wrap and refrigerate for at least 3 hours before serving.

## BEYOND COOL

- Substitute chopped red onion for the scallions, or use both!

- Some people like hot pepper sauce or red pepper flakes on couscous. Serve both on the side and see what your guests like!

- Instead of Simple Vinaigrette, try Lemon Vinaigrette. Put ¼ cup fresh lemon juice, ¾ cup olive oil, and 1 minced garlic clove in a small bowl. Whisk until blended.

# BLACK BEAN AND CORN SALAD

## ingredients

**DRESSING**

¼ cup fresh lime juice

2 cloves garlic, minced

1 teaspoon ground cumin

½ teaspoon salt

1 tablespoon chile powder

½ cup olive oil

salt and pepper

**SALAD**

2 15-ounce cans black beans, drained and rinsed

2 ears corn, kernels removed (or 1 8.5-ounce can of corn, drained)

½ cup chopped red onion

4 scallions, chopped

1 red bell pepper, chopped

¼ cup chopped cilantro leaves

## tools

measuring cups

measuring spoons

sharp knife

cutting board

can opener

strainer

mixing bowls

whisk

mixing spoon

plastic wrap

1. Combine the lime juice, garlic, cumin, salt, and chile powder in a small bowl. Whisk in the olive oil. If the **dressing** is too tart, add a little more olive oil. Add salt and pepper to taste.

2. Put the beans, corn, red onion, scallions, and bell pepper in a large mixing bowl. Add the dressing and mix well to coat. Gently mix in the cilantro.

3. Cover the bowl with plastic wrap and refrigerate for at least 3 hours before serving.

## BEYOND COOL

Make an even more colorful salad! Just before serving, add cherry tomatoes and diced avocado. Gently mix until everything is coated with dressing.

## COOL TIP

Serve this salad different ways. Wrap it in a tortilla for a burrito. Add some chips and make it a dip. Or eat it as-is for a **delicious** taste.

# CHIPOTLE CHICKEN SALAD

## ingredients

olive oil

1 pound chicken breasts

1 large red onion, cut in half,
  then sliced

1 cup mayonnaise

juice and zest from
  1 small lime

2 teaspoons adobo sauce
  (from canned chipotles)

2 cloves garlic, minced

salt and pepper

buns or lettuce

## tools

sharp knife

cutting board

measuring cups

measuring spoons

grater or zester

can opener

baking sheet

paper towels

medium mixing bowl

whisk

mixing spoon

1. Preheat the oven to 375 degrees. Lightly grease a baking sheet with olive oil.

2. Wash the chicken breasts and dry them with paper **towels**. Put the chicken on the baking sheet. Put the onion slices around the chicken. **Drizzle** olive oil over the chicken and onions.

3. Bake the chicken and onions for 30 minutes. Remove it from oven and let it cool.

4. Whisk together the mayonnaise, lime juice and **zest**, adobo sauce, and garlic in a medium mixing bowl.

5. Cube the chicken and add it to the mayonnaise mixture. Add the onions and mix until everything is well coated. Add salt and pepper to taste.

6. Serve on buns for **sandwiches**, or on lettuce for salads.

## BEYOND COOL

- For even more color and flavor, add ¼ cup chopped fresh cilantro.
- If your guests prefer spicier food, add more adobo sauce.

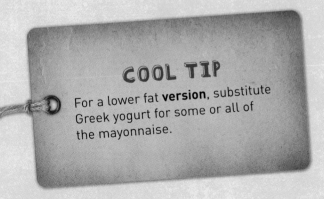

### COOL TIP

For a lower fat **version**, substitute Greek yogurt for some or all of the mayonnaise.

# ROCKIN' WALKING TACOS

## ingredients

1 pound ground beef

1 package taco seasoning mix

6 lunch-sized bags of corn chips

topping options

- shredded lettuce
- chopped tomatoes
- sliced black olives
- grated Colby-Jack or cheddar cheese
- sour cream
- salsa

## tools

sharp knife

cutting board

grater

frying pan

spatula

1. Put the ground beef in a large frying pan. Cook over medium-high heat while using a spatula to break up the meat. Cook until the meat is no longer pink. Drain the grease.

2. Add the taco seasoning to the meat and cook according to the instructions on the seasoning package.

3. Carefully open a bag of corn chips. Add some seasoned meat. Then add your choice of toppings.

## COOL TIP

Use the recipe on this page to make your own taco seasoning. Add 3 tablespoons of the homemade seasoning and ½ cup water to the meat. Cook over medium heat for about 5 minutes. Add salt to taste.

## HOMEMADE TACO SEASONING

**MAKES ABOUT 1-1½ CUPS**

ingredients

¾ cup chile powder

2 teaspoons garlic powder

2 teaspoons onion powder

1 teaspoon cayenne pepper

4 teaspoons dried oregano

2 tablespoons paprika

4 tablespoons ground cumin

2 tablespoons salt or garlic salt

2 teaspoons black pepper

1. Combine all ingredients in a bowl. Mix well.

2. Store at room temperature in a closed jar or covered container.

# HERO OF THE PICNIC SANDWICH

## ingredients

**DRESSING**

2 tablespoons red wine vinegar

1 teaspoon dried oregano

¼ cup olive oil

salt and pepper

**SANDWICH**

1 loaf French bread (18 to 20 inches long)

½ cup Italian pepper mix, finely chopped

2 cups shredded lettuce

3 tomatoes, thinly sliced

½ pound salami, sliced

½ pound pepperoni, sliced

½ pound provolone cheese, sliced

## tools

measuring cups

measuring spoons

serrated knife

cutting board

small mixing bowl

whisk

plastic wrap

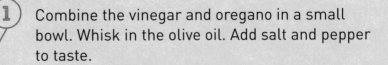

1. Combine the vinegar and oregano in a small bowl. Whisk in the olive oil. Add salt and pepper to taste.

2. Lay three long pieces of plastic wrap on the work surface so they **overlap**.

3. Cut the bread in half lengthwise. Put the bottom half on the plastic wrap.

4. Spread the Italian pepper mix over the bread. Put the lettuce evenly over the pepper mix and top with tomatoes. **Drizzle** half the **dressing** on top.

5. Arrange the meat slices evenly over the tomatoes. Add the cheese slices.

6. Drizzle the rest of the dressing over the inside of the top of the bread. Place the top of the bread on the cheese.

7. Wrap the plastic wrap tightly around the **sandwich**. Refrigerate for 1 to 4 hours before serving. Cut into 8 pieces.

## COOL TIP

You can make any dressing in a jar with a tight-fitting lid. Put the ingredients in the jar. Cover the jar and shake until the dressing is well blended. Add salt and pepper to taste.

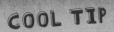

# SAVORY OVEN-FRIED CHICKEN

## ingredients

10 chicken drumsticks
1 quart buttermilk
non-stick cooking spray
2 cups dried bread crumbs
1 teaspoon salt
1 teaspoon black pepper
1 teaspoon paprika
½ cup mayonnaise

## tools

measuring cups
measuring spoons
paper towels
mixing bowls
plastic wrap
baking sheet
plastic zipper bag
whisk
tongs
sharp knife

1. Wash the drumsticks and dry them with paper **towels**. Put them in a large mixing bowl. Pour 3 cups buttermilk over the chicken. Make sure all the drumsticks get coated with buttermilk. Cover the bowl with plastic wrap and refrigerate overnight.

2. When you are ready to bake the chicken, preheat the oven to 400 degrees. Coat the baking sheet with non-stick cooking spray.

3. Put the bread crumbs, salt, pepper, and paprika in a plastic zipper bag. Seal the bag and shake it to mix the ingredients.

4. Whisk the mayonnaise and ½ cup buttermilk together in a medium mixing bowl.

5. Coat a drumstick with the mayonnaise mixture. Put it in the bag with bread crumb mixture. Close the bag and shake gently to coat the chicken.

6. Place the drumstick on the baking sheet.

7. Repeat steps 5 and 6 with the other drumsticks. Bake for 30 minutes. Turn the drumsticks over and bake for 25 to 30 more minutes. Test for doneness by piercing thickest part of meat with a sharp knife. If the juices are clear, the chicken is done. It is **delicious** served either hot or cold!

## COOL TIP

For a crunchier coating, use 1 cup Panko bread crumbs and 1 cup dried bread crumbs. Panko bread crumbs are **available** in the Asian sections of many **grocery stores**.

# FRESH-SQUEEZED LEMONADE

HOT STUFF!  SUPER SHARP!

## ingredients

1 cup sugar
6 to 8 lemons

## tools

measuring cups
small saucepan
mixing spoon
zester or grater
strainer
2-quart pitcher
sharp knife
cutting board
juicer

1. Make a simple syrup. Put the sugar and 1 cup water in a small saucepan. Bring it to a boil and stir until the sugar **dissolves**.

2. Remove the pan from the heat. Let the syrup cool for 30 minutes. Add **zest** from 4 lemons. Refrigerate overnight.

3. Strain the syrup into a **pitcher**.

4. Juice the lemons until you have 1 cup of fresh lemon juice. Put the lemon juice in the pitcher. Add water to fill the pitcher. Stir. If the lemonade is too sour, add more sugar and stir until the sugar dissolves.

5. Serve in glasses with ice and lemon slices.

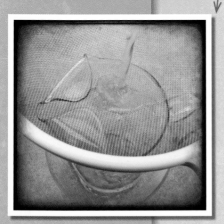

# GLOSSARY

available – able to be had or used.

delicious – very pleasing to taste or smell.

dessert – a sweet food, such as fruit, ice cream, or pastry, served after a meal.

dissolve – to mix with a liquid so that it becomes part of the liquid.

dressing – a sauce that is used in salads.

drizzle – to pour in a thin stream.

efficient – able to do something without wasting time, money, or energy.

fluff – to loosen or separate using a fork.

garbage – something you throw away, such as food waste.

glossary – a list of the hard or unusual words found in a book.

grater – a tool with sharp-edged holes.

grocery store – a store that sells mostly food items.

option – something you can choose.

overlap – to lie partly on top of something.

permission – when a person in charge says it's okay to do something.

pitcher – a container with a handle used to hold and pour liquids.

prep – short for preparation, the work done before starting to make a recipe, such as washing fruits and vegetables, measuring, cutting, peeling, and grating.

sandwich – two pieces of bread with a filling, such as meat, cheese, or peanut butter, between them.

supervision – the act of watching over or directing others.

technique – a method or style in which something is done.

towel – a cloth or paper used for cleaning or drying.

utensil – a tool used to prepare or eat food.

version – a different form or type from the original.

zest – small pieces of the peel of a citrus fruit, made by rubbing the fruit with a zester or grater.

# WEB SITES

To learn more about cool cooking, visit ABDO Publishing Company online at www.abdopublishing.com. Web sites about cool cooking are featured on our Book Links page. These links are monitored and updated to provide the most current information available.

# INDEX